DAY OUT

with

Derek Jones and Gwyn Richards

ABSON BOOKS · ABSON · WICK · BRISTOL

by arrangement with the

BBC

ACKNOWLEDGEMENTS

We would like to thank the colleagues who worked with us at various times during the making of the Day Out programmes:

Producer:	Keith Sheather
Director:	Ruth Lovell
Producer's Assistant:	Margaret Darch
Cameramen:	Mike Giddings, Clive North, David Saunders, Steve Wagstaff
Sound:	Tom Brown, Peter Copeland, Ron Dauben, Edward Johnson
Film Editors:	Colin Cradock, Bernard Goodsall, Andrew Johnston, Bish Mehay, Jim Tobin, Richard Steenhuis

BOOK CREDITS

Photographs:	Clive North
Maps:	Eve Woodbury-Eggins

First published in Great Britain in 1977
by ABSON BOOKS, Abson, Wick, Bristol by arrangement with The British Broadcasting Corporation.

ISBN 0 902920 30 8

CONTENTS

INTRODUCTION

AFTER one of the 'Day Out' programmes on B.B.C. television, one lady wrote to say how much she'd enjoyed watching the walk around so-and-so, because it had told her something she didn't know about the place – and she lived there! Since we'd embarked on the series without knowing what kind of response they would get, that was the kind of testimonial we needed!

The idea was that we two presenters would take it in turns, week by week, to do exactly what so many people enjoy doing for a nice day out – hopping into the car and finding somewhere interesting slightly off the beaten track.

Producer Keith Sheather, whose idea the series was, set about listing some of the places which fell with a bump into that category, places like Shaftesbury, Langport, Wotton-under-Edge and Frome, the town which one of our colleagues described in a graphic phrase, when saying how much he'd enjoyed Derek's stroll around the place, 'you know, up until now, Frome to me was just a gear change on the A361!' With director Ruth Lovell, who took over responsibility for some of the programmes, the series began to take shape.

But when he gave the go-ahead for the programmes, James Dewar, the B.B.C.'s Regional Television Manager in the West made just one stipulation – keep it simple. No complicated shooting schedules and the circus that tends to go with them. After all, how many people take a large crowd of cameramen and technicians with them when they go out for the day!

So it was a case of back to basic principles, putting us in worthwhile pictorial situations, wherever possible with a good story to tell (you'd be surprised how many we dug up) and simply letting one camera follow us, come what may, through the streets, lanes and footpaths, historic houses, churches, castles and front parlours of these twelve West Country towns and villages.

And we discovered how essential it was to 'keep it simple'. Every time you move a film crew from one location to another, even a small one, it means lost time, as all the gear has to be loaded up into vehicles, transported a mile or so, unloaded all over again and set up ready to film in the next situation. And with only two days to get everything in the can, we hardly had enough time to allow for a shower of rain. And yet, willy-nilly, we found very often that we could only move at the pace of life of the place we were in and the people who lived there. That was the beauty of it, really. Yes, we filmed the people and the places, but we also found we were filming *atmosphere*, loads of it, and we believe that lovely 'feel' about the locations comes through in the programmes.

Young onlookers we found were seldom shy in putting the question, 'What you doing then, mister?' which usually led to chats about this and that and another new friend along the way. Kindness we found everywhere too, the ever-acceptable cuppas from folk who had no part in the films; the willingness of householders and shop keepers to allow us to film from vantage points in or on their premises (even shutting up shop for a few minutes); above all, the interest, '. . . glad you've come to see us Gwyn . . . hope you like our town, Derek!'

We were glad – and yes, we liked them. We hope you do, too.

DEVIZES

with Gwyn Richards

IF I HAD to take a man from Mars to two sanctuaries of all that is English, then I suppose I would take him to a pub and a market, in either order. Furthermore, I would take him to Devizes, to find the best of both worlds.

For three hundred years, Thursday has always been market day in Devizes, so naturally, that was the day we went there. I got there very early, but I still wasn't early enough to beat one man unloading piles of fresh fruit and vegetables from his lorry. Then, as the early sunshine caught the marvellous statue of Ceres, goddess of the fields, on top of the Corn Exchange, the rest of the market traders started putting up stalls all around me.

There is a covered market in the Shambles, by the way, which opens on Saturdays too, selling everything from fresh fish to homemade sweets. And in the market place itself, you can sample Strong's cheesecake, made to a secret recipe for over a hundred and fifty years. Then there's fresh baked bread and lardy cake in the pastry shop down the road, pulled hot from the ovens before your very eyes. Whatever else you do, don't expect to go to Devizes and lose weight!

Walking through this fascinating but somewhat sleepy little town, it's incredible to discover that here in the 12th Century Roger de Caen, Chancellor of England under Henry Ist, and Bishop of Salisbury, built the mightiest fortress in Europe. The town, in fact, grew around it, and even though the castle was destroyed all but one tower by Cromwell's armies after the Battle of Roundway Down, the town's mediaeval street pattern, in a semi-circle round the castle, hasn't changed. That's one of the features about Devizes I found very attractive – you feel that time has stood still. The castle is now privately owned, with a beautifully mown moat!

Devizes has been a garrison town for centuries, from

DEVIZES: Little Brittox

the time of General Wolfe to the G.I.s during the last war, but now the army is pulling out. This end of an epoch will change Devizes but, as always, it will dust itself off and start all over again.

The fine folk of this town have for over 200 years been weaned on some of the best and strongest beer brewed in England. Run by the same family, they own almost every pub in the place and round about, and deliver their brew by means of horse and dray. The clip-clopping Shire horses with their tinkling brasses can be seen most days of the week.

On the market stands the Bear, a famous old coaching inn, which on market days seems to be open *all* day! It was founded four hundred years ago and was the home in the 18th Century of the young Thomas Lawrence, an undoubted genius who was making portraits of the famous people who stayed at the inn when he was only five. He later fulfilled his promise by becoming one of the greatest portrait painters this country has produced and President of the Royal Academy of Art. The inn still possesses some of his early drawings.

Unlike the Bear, many half-timbered buildings were pulled down and replaced by Georgian brick, but not St John's Alley, a half-hidden row of overhanging Elizabethan merchants' houses, now the subject of an urgent restoration appeal.

In Long Street the Museum contains one of the most famous prehistoric geological and archaeological collections in the country, including the massive cremation urn found at Stonehenge and borne back in triumph in a pony and trap!

All roads seem to lead back to the market and on the way, I was glad I spent a little time at St John's church, which is probably almost as old as the castle. In the churchyard there is a slim pillar, erected as 'an awful warning' upon the deaths of four young people drowned while boating on the Sabbath. And on the market cross is an inscription spelling out another dire threat! Beware the story of Ruth Pierce, who swore that she may be struck down dead if she had not paid her fair share of a bargain. She suffered exactly that fate, dropping down dead on the spot. In her fist were found the three pennies she owed!

As for me, I owe Devizes my thanks for a good day out.

DEVIZES

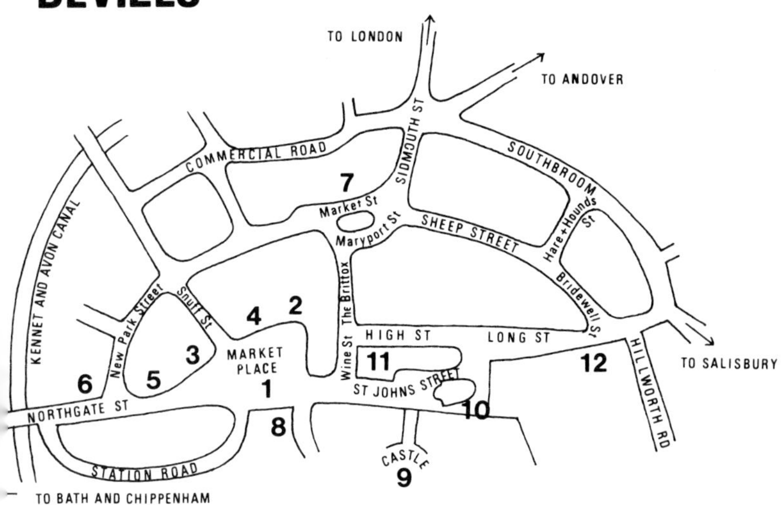

Market Place. Central meeting place of farmers and shoppers since the 13th century. Street market here every Thursday.

Shambles. In the middle ages butchers sold their meat here. Now this covered market sells a variety of goods on Thursdays and Saturdays.

The Black Swan Yard. 12 noon every Thursday sale of cattle, sheep, and general produce in yard through archway of this old inn.

Restaurant. Home of local delicacy made from secret recipe – Devizes cheesecake.

Bakery. Pies, various, sold here but lardie cake a speciality.

Brewery. For over 200 years this family concern has dominated the town – famous for the strength of its beer and its splendid horse-drawn drays.

7. **Great Porch House.** Standing in Monday Market Street and built in the 15th century when this street was the scene of yet another weekly market.
8. **The Bear Hotel.** Dominating corner of the market square, this hostelry has provided for travellers for nearly four centuries.
9. **Castle.** Once the location of the biggest castle in Europe. Remains now privately occupied. Not open to the public.
10. **St. John's Court.** Leads to St. John's Church.
11. **St. John's Alley.** This cobbled alley once the home of medieval guild halls and the spot where many traders sold their goods.
12. **Museum.** Also contains fine library and is the headquarters of the Wiltshire Archaeological Society.

STROUD
with Derek Jones

My first real view of Stroud was from the vantage point provided by the imposing tower sitting squarely in the trees atop of Rodborough Common. From there, in the tower, I looked out over the town with its industrial artery following the banks of the River Frome in the valley; the old terraced housing on the higher parts, relics of a cottage industry way of life and the new housing estates which perform the same purpose of keeping the workers near to their employment.

That tower on Rodborough Common is known as Rodborough Fort and despite its battlements it never was a fort, but rather a sham, built more than two hundred years ago by one George Hawker as a place to live, or perhaps a place to look down on the town and the green hills of the Cotswold beyond dotted white with sheep.

Hawker was a clothier and the reputation of Stroud has long been woven into the woollen trade. There were the sheep heavy with wool on their backs on those grassy green hills; here was water in the valley so necessary in all the processes of the wool trade. To-day only two of the mills are still in the wool business although some of the other original buildings have survived and are unmistakably mills of days gone by. They've been snapped up for industrial purposes far removed from wool, but there's no denying their past.

The Museum is naturally, a good point to get a real idea of the importance of Stroud in the wool trade. There's a picture hanging there of the town, very much the sort of view I had from high up on Rodborough Common, but with one important difference. The picture is old and dark and dare I say in need of some cleaning, but standing out like beacons in the fields around the town are vivid splashes of scarlet. This is no accidental 'splodging' on the part of the artist, but Stroud as it was.

STROUD: Shambles

Those patches of red were the famous Stroud Scarlet stretched out to dry after dying, stretched out on tenter-hooks.

To-day the cloth is dried on a huge machine, all rollers and gears and heat in the factory, a tentering machine.

That Stroud Scarlet we've all seen, much more recently during the Jubilee celebrations, as the immaculate lines of the Brigade of Guards have gone through their seemingly impossible drill manoeuvres with the usual expected precision. Their jackets are made of Stroud Scarlet, a cloth so closely woven and so beautifully soft that rain runs off it without any artificial proofing.

The wool factory of Strachan's still produce it but not to-day from the contented Cotswold sheep on the nearby hillsides, but from specially bred Merino sheep in South Africa and Australia. As I was told in Stroud, sheep bred for meat don't produce good wool, and sheep bred for wool aren't much good for eating. The factory just about keeps up with the Ministry of Defence needs for Stroud Scarlet, but it has more expensive lines like the green baize for billiard tables, and if it came to the truth of the matter, I could be very much at home in a topcoat made from the pure Kashmir – or should I say, cashmere – that they run off for the high class tailors of London's West End.

Edwin Budding of Stroud got his idea for the lawn mower from a new rotary cutter installed in a woollen mill to cut the nap on the cloth, and I found it a tremendous surprise that the cutting blades on the mower we push and curse round our gardens to-day are exactly the same as those on the original patented by Edwin Budding in 1830. Mind you, he did have the foresight to add a pulling handle as well as a pusher. That was so that your wife could help too.

You can get away from wool for a while in Stroud but not for long. The quaint church looking for all the world like a church in the Alps resting on the hillside outside

STROUD

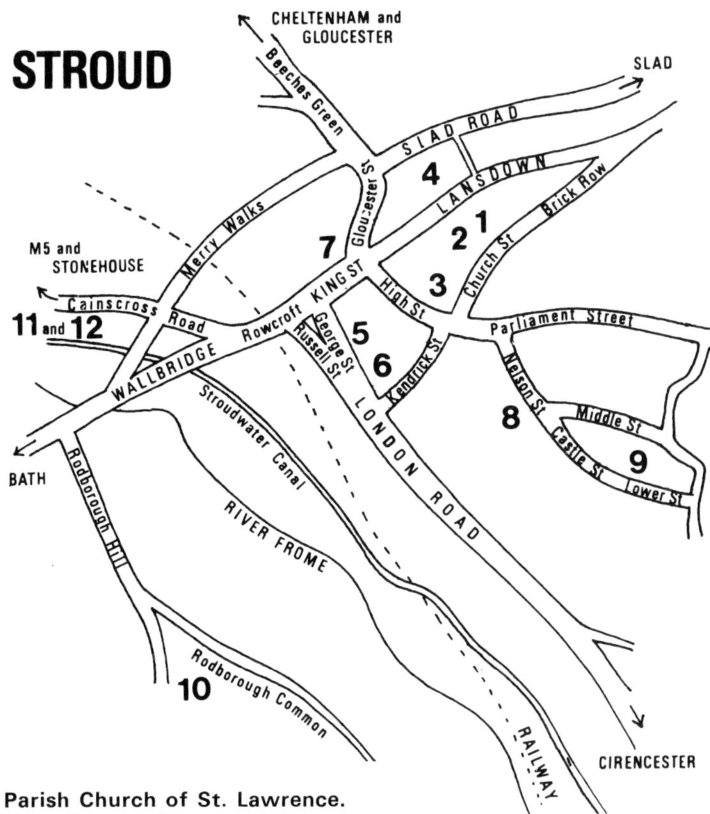

Parish Church of St. Lawrence. Actor Edmund Kean married local girl Mary Chambres 1808.

Lieutenant Delmont's Grave. Look for it in south-west corner of graveyard.

Shambles. Old meat market with fine Elizabethan house, John Wesley preached here.

Museum. Look out for early lawn mower, artefacts of the wool trade, awesome model of Megalosaurus.

Congregational Chapel. Fine classical building 1837.

Subscription Rooms. Impressive facade, built by public subscription 1833, after Stroud enfranchised 1832.

7. **'Railway Time' Clock.** On corner of King Street and Gloucester Street.
8. **Black Boy Clock.** Recently restored 18th century Jack clock on wall of Teacher's Centre.
9. **'Top Town'.** Good example of surviving old Stroud.
10. **Rodborough Common.** Fine view of Rodborough Fort and Stroud valley.
11. **Woollen Mills.** Excellent examples to be found along river Frome valley and restored Stroudwater Canal.
12. **All Saints Church, Selsey.** Stained glass windows by William Morris, Ford Maddox Brown, Burne-Jones Rossetti.

the town at Selsley is a case in point. You soon discover that wool was responsible.

Sir Samuel Marling had it built in 1862 after he'd paid a visit to a church in the Austrian Tyrol. He, of course, was a wealthy clothier.

But have a look too at other things. The Railway Time clock on the corner of King Street. It's the sort of device that brings us down to earth with a bang. Just think, when we all relied on sun dials to keep us betimes, our time in the West would be different to that in London for instance. In Stroud the difference would have been 8½ minutes – 8½ minutes behind London time. But trains didn't carry sun dials and the timetables were based on London time. So Railway Time clocks were set to London time, so that we could catch our trains which apparently were very punctual in those days. The date on the Stroud clock is 1858.

Time came to an end for one man in the town just over 50 years earlier, when Joseph Francis Delmont died. Delmont's grave is tucked away under the dark yew trees in a corner of the parish church of St Lawrence. A small memorial tablet records barely that this officer, for he was a Lieutenant in His Majesty's 82nd Regiment, died on 18th August 1807, and having done your arithmetic you realise that he was but 22 years of age.

He could have died in battle maybe. In a way, he did. In a personal man-to-man battle which was the last such ever to take place in this country. A duel. Pistols at dawn and that sort of thing. It seems Delmont fell out over some chance remark for which he refused to apologise with a fellow officer. The twist to the story is that Delmont lived for five days after the duel, and claimed that he was shot in the back. A macabre story maybe and one that gives Stroud a certain claim to fame, but then what town, anywhere, hasn't got skeletons that rattle in the cupboard now and again.

WOTTON-UNDER-EDGE

with Gwyn Richards

Not only does Wotton-under-Edge – or Wut-nuder-idge as the locals say – offer the nicest possibilities for a day out, it also has become a very attractive proposition for the commuters, the people who work perhaps in Bristol, but actually live in the green fields and on the Cotswold hillsides. How has this come about? Why, the motorway. Until the M5 was built, curving less than five miles away, Wotton remained very much what it had always been, a town founded on the woollen industry, tucked under the escarpment, minding its own business.

So, climb up one of the hills around the town first. It's good for your legs and for your senses, because from here you can look right across the beautiful Vale of Berkeley. Wotton was for centuries part of the manor of Berkeley Castle, where Edward II was so nastily done to death.

Streams run down into the town from springs rising in the hills. Down the valleys, little white cottages are sprinkled like sugar lumps, once the humble dwellings of workers in the woollen mills, now quite often reappearing as the character residences of the commuters.

Nowhere is very far from anywhere in a town of Wotton's size of course, so I suggest you begin your visit to the town itself in Old Town, round the parish church. This was the probable site of the Saxon settlement of Wudeton, mentioned in the Domesday book, and destroyed by fire in the reign of bad King John. The church of St Mary the Virgin dates from this period, 13th Century, and so does the oldest house in Wotton, the Ram Inn virtually next door, where the stonemasons and carpenters lodged who built the church.

Make your way now to the Chipping, in the middle of Wotton. This is where you begin to get a taste of the nice atmosphere of this little Cotswold town. This is the old market place. There are some beautiful little cottages around and the old Chipping Manor has been superbly restored. But as you walk out into Market Street, notice how the whole of the East side has been restored from total dereliction to a faithful copy of the original, winning for the local builder whose creation it was, a national Civic Trust award, and rightly.

On the corner is the Tolsey House clock. The Tolsey was the market toll house, where the aldermen who administered the market, the feoffees, held the Court of Pie Powder to try those luckless ones who broke the market rules. There's even a cell under the floor.

Below the clock, the rest of High Street becomes Long Street, and I loved this little shopping centre (apart from one or two unlovely shop fronts), many buildings having roofs of ancient Cotswold stone tiles and higgledy-piggledy roof lines. The upper storeys would often have contained looms where families wove cloth for the merchants. Take a look at Berkeley House, a fine Jacobean building. All the shopkeepers I met, by the way, and the local people, were friendly and ready for a chat, particularly on their favourite subject – Wotton-under-Edge!

Lower down are the Hugh Perry almshouses, built in 1634 under the will of a local lad who rose to become High Sheriff of London Town, no less. Through the arch visitors are welcome to walk into the charming courtyard and pass the time of day with the residents, or spend a quiet moment in the little chapel.

But dominating the whole town, just a short walk up the hill, is another house of worship, the Tabernacle Church, which now has a quite different use. On its floor, under the bust of the church's founder, a fiery preacher called Roland Hill, is a monument to those pagan conquerors, the Romans. The new owner of the church has painstakingly recreated an exact copy of the famous Woodchester mosaic pavement a few miles away, which is only uncovered once every ten years. What's more, the Wotton copy will be as complete as the Romans

WOTTON-UNDER-EDGE: Tolsey Clock (High Street)

would have known it, and visitors will be able to gaze down on it from the balcony.

You'll make your own little discoveries in Wotton, I know, but before you leave, make a point of seeing New Mill. It's down in the fields below the town, but is the last remaining working textile mill. The old building is a magnificent early 19th century factory building, which employed generations of men, women and children in the woollen industry before the onward march of the Industrial Revolution forced it into decline. Now part of the premises manufactures modern narrow fabrics.

That's Wotton-under-Edge. I know you'll like it, as we did. But be prepared – it grows on you! It might be the beginning of a long lasting relationship!

WOTTON-UNDER-EDGE

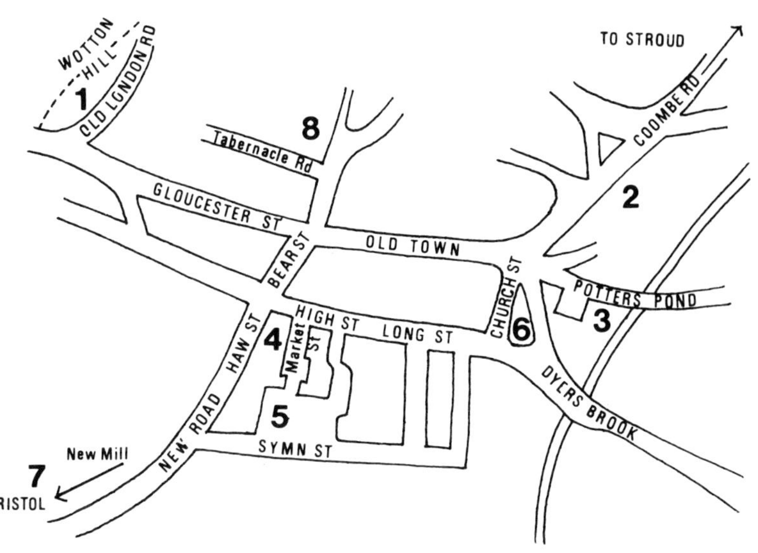

Wotton Hill. The Jubilee Clump on top of this hill (approached by foot from the old London road) dominates the town.

The Church. The Parish Church of St. Mary the Virgin stands in old Town. One of its treasures is an organ built for King George I who presented it to St. Martin in the Fields. It was brought to Wotton in the early part of the 19th century.

The Ram Inn. Wotton's oldest house where carpenters and stonemasons lived while building the church.

Market Street and Tolsey House. A considerable part of Market Street has been reconstructed to preserve its original character. At the end stands the ancient Tolsey House or Market Toll House.

5. **The Chipping.** Or old market place – now good car park.
6. **Perry & Dawes Almshouses.** One of three sets of almshouses in the town. Set in peaceful quadrangle with lawns and little chapel these were provided by Hugh Perry and Thomas Dawes. Recently reconstructed and modernised, visitors welcome.
7. **New Mills.** Approx. 1 mile from town. Now only working textile mill left in area (not open to public).
8. **Tabernacle Church.** Church unused for many years but now renovated and contains a re-creation of the Woodchester Roman Pavement.

SHERBORNE
with Gwyn Richards

As I walked across ancient flagstones, along castle walls and under archways a thousand years old, I felt as if a million pairs of eyes were watching me. Ringing round the old stone town were the footsteps of all those who had gone before. There is an awful lot of history in Sherborne!

For thousands and thousands of boys of course, Sherborne means only one thing – school. For centuries the town has lived cheek by jowl with one of England's most famous public schools, Sherborne School. At the beginning of each term, thither the schoolboys went, leaving home behind in pleasure or in pain. In fact since Saxon times, Sherborne has been what one headteacher described to me as 'an education machine' and today supports six senior schools and a satchel full of primary ones.

There was no pain for me, anyway, in my visit to this little north Dorset town. One of its pleasures is that you can walk almost anywhere, even into the school's old courtyard where in term time the boys gather between lessons. But the really amazing thing about Sherborne is its Abbey. It's still standing! Unlike King Alfred's great Abbey at Shaftesbury, reduced to some picturesque piles of stones, Sherborne Abbey, founded by Bishop Aldhelm in 705, has been at the centre of the town's life for over twelve hundred years. Not always peacefully, however. There was such a squabble between the Abbey monks and the townspeople at one time that the roof was set on fire by a flaming arrow. Inside the Choir, you can still see red scorch marks on the walls. Today the Abbey still dominates the town.

On the war memorial outside the Abbey is a plaque commemorating the deaths of twenty civilians in the town during the last war. A formation of German bombers jettisoned their load over Sherborne when harried by R.A.F. fighters. The Abbey escaped, and the one school

SHERBORNE: Abbey

to be hit was empty.

To walk through these sometimes steep and narrow little streets today is a pure pleasure. Towards the bottom of the main street is a curious pagoda-like construction called the Conduit, which was once the monk's washing house at the Abbey. It's been used as a penny bank and even a reading room. Now it looks to me like a mediaeval greenhouse without the glass. Spend time in the town; there are good shops and plenty of places to eat, drink and generally refresh yourself. But don't linger too long, because I want to show you Sherborne's two castles, associated with the poignant story of one of the great heroes of our maritime nation.

Sir Walter Raleigh, at the height of his favour at the court of Queen Elizabeth Ist, begged her to give him an estate. She eventually wrung out of the Bishop of Salisbury the old castle of Sherborne, built by the Chancellor of England in the 12th Century, Roger de Caen. With it went manors and lands. Unfortunately Raleigh found it uninhabitable, and so half a mile away, across a beautiful valley, he built a superb mansion which, with later additions, still stands today, and is known as Sherborne's second castle. The first castle also stands, but only as a ruin, and a spectacular one at that, destroyed by Cromwell's armies during the Civil War.

Raleigh's downfall came when his heart and then later, his tongue, ran away with him. The story is that at court he recklessly fell in love with one of the Queen's ladies-in-waiting, Bess Throckmorton. There is a painting in the castle which probably shows them dressed in silver surrounded by the whole court with the Queen on a sedan chair. To make matters worse, the girl was pregnant. When she discovered the truth, Elizabeth flew into a rage and banished them, Walter to the Tower and Bess to Sherborne. But she forgave him and for years after, they lived happily at Sherborne where Bess bore him a son.

Raleigh's personal disaster came when he was accused, rightly or wrongly, of plotting against the new King, Scottish James Ist. Arrested, he was again consigned to the Tower, his lands, including Sherborne, forfeited. Eventually he was beheaded. Only in recent years was an unknown will by Raleigh found in the possession of the Digby family, who have lived in the house for over four hundred years.

Sherborne is beautiful, even though some of its memories are sad. Enjoy your day out.

SHERBORNE

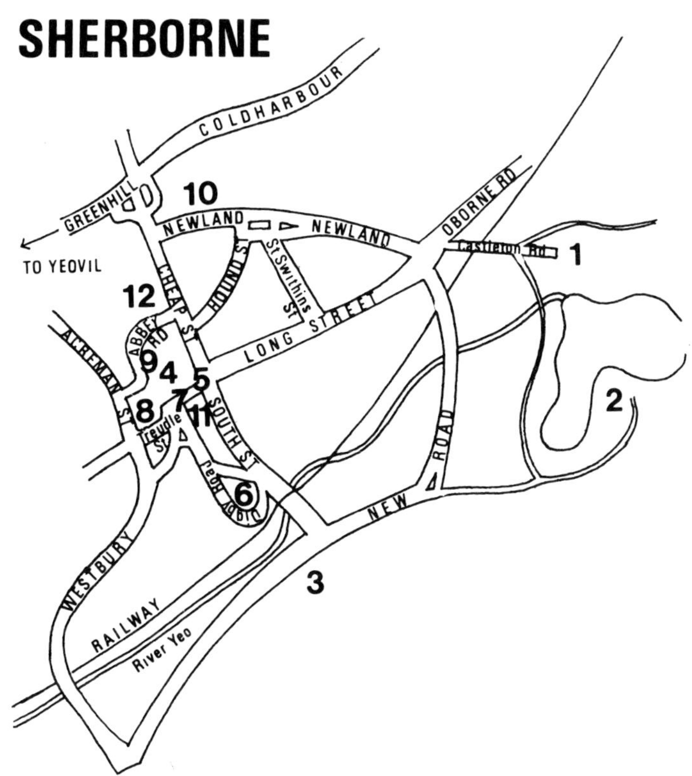

1. **Sherborne Castle.** Old castle ruins open to public (Department of the Environment).
2. **Sherborne Castle.** New castle open to public on certain days.
3. **Terrace.** Impressive view of town from Terrace playing fields.
4. **Abbey.**
5. **Monks' Conduit.** Lower Cheap Street.
6. **Pageant Gardens.** Laid out from proceeds of 1905 Sherborne Pageant, the 'mother of pageants'.
7. **War Memorial.**
8. **Almshouse.** 15th century with fine Flemish Triptych, painted around 1475.
9. **Sherborne School.**
10. **Lord Digby's School.** 18th century home of Portman family. Fine murals by Sir James Thornhill depicting legend of Calydonian boar, now Girls' Grammar School.
11. **Old Church House.** Medieval building in Half Moon Street, its upper storey once one long room.
12. **Cheap Street.** Main shopping street with many interesting buildings.

WATCHET

with Derek Jones

Most of us approach this traditional holiday area by leaving the Motorway at Bridgwater, and then head for the hills along the winding meandering A39 with its collections of communities and traditional pubs along the way that set us in holiday mood, apart from the fact that all along the route we've been stuck behind a large lorry loaded down with bright red brand new farm tractors, with very little chance of passing with safety. Then, glory be, that heavy nuisance has turned off 'our road' and taken a side turning to the right. We are probably so overjoyed at having lost the lorry that we fail to notice that the signpost to the road it has taken points to Watchet. Follow one of those lorries one of these days and you'll be in for a pleasant surprise. The legend goes that long ago a Celtic missionary came into Watchet by sea. Decumen was his name. He had a chilly reception and the reception committee, as was traditional in those days did the only thing they could with unwelcome invaders; they lopped off his head. Decumen calmly picked up his head and put it back on his shoulders. Miracles are the currency of religious conversion and the more improbable the story the more converts join the flock. Whatever else St Decumen did, he apparently established a Christian settlement on a hill above the town on the site of the present Parish Church, the Church of St Decumen. Frankly, I found the climb up the hill to the Church enough of a marathon without having previously gone through all the troubles of that distant Saint, but perhaps men were tougher mortals in those days. As if to underline the difficulties of attending worship to-day up that steep hill, there is the most beautiful little chapel in the upper storey of the old Market House in the town where Holy Communion is celebrated twice a week. When we were there making our

WATCHET: Lighthouse and Cliff

film, plans were well advanced to use the ground floor of the Market House as a local museum; there could be no more fitting place for it.

It was down here, among the holidaymakers who've found for themselves the charm of the town, that I fell in love with it. Walk down Swain Street towards the Market Place, and you look out across an expanse of mud and rub your eyes with disbelief. Is that a ship sitting there on the far side, high and dry with not a foot of water under her keel? It is a ship, there is no water and this is the harbour.

Talk to a local and you'll probably be told that they take the plug out twice a day. The penny will soon drop as you remember about the high tides of the Bristol Channel.

The fact is there was a port and a town here long before Bristol was ever thought of. It was a natural harbour, Watchet's, formed by the ceaseless erosion of the sea on one hand and the gouging out of the bed of the River Washford on the other. According to records the River was once as wide as the Thames at Westminster. But to-day, as you look over the mud of the harbour bed you might just notice a trickle of water of serpent-like shape navigating a path through the mud. That's the river. Go away for a while as I did, sample a lunch in one of the welcoming pubs, or a snack at the Corner Cafe (their home-baked bread and their doughnuts are delicious) and come back when they've put the plug back in and the harbour has filled, and see the change.

The fact is that here is a busy working port. Those tractors on the back of the lorry you cursed earlier, are now in the hold of a ship destined for Spain, Portugal or the Azores.

The last figures I saw showed just how successful a business they have in this quiet town. Forty million pounds worth of exports in a year and that means considerable harbour dues, something like £30,000 a year.

WATCHET

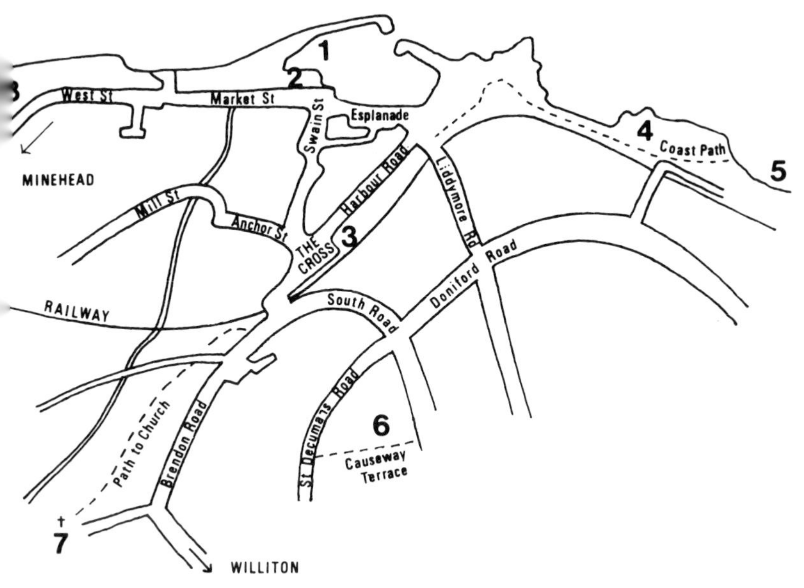

. **Harbour.** Good views from west pier, esplanade, and east coast path.

. **Market House.** Junction of Swain Street and Market Street.

. **Watchet Station.** Now a stopping point for the West Somerset Railway.

. **Cliffs.** Can be reached from harbour by coast path.

. **Helwell Bay.** Hunting ground for ammonites and other fossil remains, good sands.

6. **Causeway Terrace.** Unique row of 18th century farm workers' cottages built with front doors at the back so that the big house at the top of hill didn't look on lines of washing.
7. **St. Decumen's Church.** See also St. Decumen's well nearby.
8. **Lime Kilns.** Remains still visible, lime used to repair dungeons of Dunster Castle 1405, and to build Eddystone Lighthouse.

The docks then are the heart of Watchet, it's always been that way and it's here as a ship clears the narrow harbour mouth on the high tide that folk stop their labours and see her safely out to sea. I joined them and watched and waved as they did.

But I had to tear myself away and look at the fossil remains in the cliffs and on the foreshore, an archaeologists' paradise; to look at the old lime kilns and wander along high cliff-tops among an extraordinary hatch of butterflies that welcomed my day out in Watchet. May you find there the pleasure that I found, and more. You might even find the view that Coleridge found when he wrote 'The Ancient Mariner'.

> '*The ship was cheered, the harbour cleared,*
> *Merrily did we drop*
> *Below the kirk, below the hill,*
> *Below the lighthouse top.*'

FROME
with Derek Jones

'Which is the way to Frome?' (rhyming it with home) asks the lost traveller of a local worthy. He's had this one before has our worthy and puts them right with a well rounded Somerset delivery of the correct and proper form of the name of the town. They reach Frome do our travellers and from that moment on the place is doomed. Not only has it caught them out with its name, but it's a bottleneck – a series of steep slopes leading into a hollow and steep slopes up the other side. That's not the way I remember it, because I stopped to explore it, and it's a great pity that more folk couldn't be persuaded to do the same.

Frome is a walking town. When those very important people in very important places produce new designs for towns for us to live in they seem to put down one central area for shops shaped like a piece from a jig-saw puzzle and put on it a 'Pedestrians Only' sign. Sometimes they even remember to add the adjacent piece of the puzzle and put a smaller sign beside it. That one may indicate 'Car Park'. The modern aid to modern living has been born in a grand plan. But Frome, or at least the older parts of the town, are just like that and it didn't come about through any planner's great design, it just happened. Tumbling narrow streets and alleys and lanes that radiate out from the Market Place like the spokes of a well-founded wheel on a solid farm cart. Some of the spokes have been widened over the years just enough to allow the traveller to pass, just; others have been left as they were and as you walk up or down their slopes you can imagine yourself transported back in time to more leisured days when making a purchase involved a chat and a barter rather than to-day's flurried impersonal supermarket way of living and buying. Cheap Street is a case in point. You just can't get a car in there, and if you want to see it and its beautiful old buildings, you just have to hoof it. It's the living example of what a medieval street really was with no two buildings alike, each one a gem in its own right. Half-timbered houses with the first floors overhanging the front doors.

I found myself so much in the past that it seemed natural to look above as I meandered along to make sure that I wasn't due for a bucket of slops over my head from an upstairs window. The feeling is heightened and emphasised by the stream which gurgles down the gulley in the middle of the street. What better way, after all, of keeping a walkway free of filth? To-day it's neat and clean and tidy. A beautiful bit of the past that has hardly changed over the years and nor for that matter have many of the others like Gentle Street, cobbled, elegant and gracious. Here too, it was easy to imagine oneself back in another time.

There's only one thing will drag you away from Gentle Street and the highly desirable properties that have settled in impossible angles and shapes into its hillside, and that is the Parish Church of St John the Baptist half way down the hill. The first impression is just another church until you realise that the ornate carvings alongside it seem completely our of character with an English churchyard; a tremendously elaborate sculpture depicting the Road to Calvary. And spare a glance too, for the tomb of Thomas Ken, Bishop of Bath and Wells, buried discreetly under the east end of the church.

Ken it was who fell foul of the monarchy when he refused to swear allegiance to William of Orange and so was to lose his bishopric.

Everywhere I went in Frome a new experience unfolded before me. Walk some of the roads – Catherine Hill for instance – and you wonder how on earth heavy carts and carriages could possibly have negotiated the inclines and bends of the old main streets leading into the town.

There's one area of Frome though where the imagin-

FROME: Cheap Street

ation really does run riot, not because of its history and its undoubted claim to fame, but because of what has been allowed to happen to it. Here in the Trinity area you might think yourself in a town hastily evacuated after some deadly plague. Where once were windows and doors are now sheets of rusting, galvanised iron; old hinges creak a chorus of ghostly sounds; cats stalk the dusty ruins. This is a relic of the days of cottage industries, of weavers working in return for a roof over their heads and at most street corners the faded names of old pub signs show where the men found their refreshment. But until it's decided what to do with these old streets and houses time is taking its toll. Some say the whole lot should be razed to the ground and redeveloped; others would see each and every cottage lovingly restored for after all, here is what they claim to be the biggest surviving collection of 17th century industrial dwellings in the country. But despite this one controversial topic, Frome is a happy town. Like anywhere else this controversy keeps the town on its toes and makes its folk talk and think about the place in which they live and work and play, and in Frome I sensed a strong community feeling and a pride. To me those two factors alone are enough to make it a worthwhile place in which to plant one's roots.

FROME

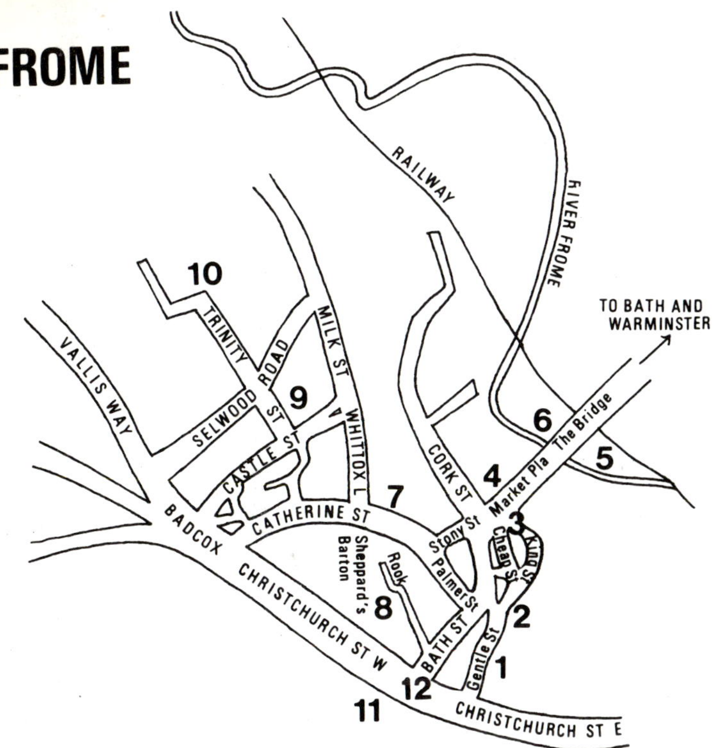

1. **Gentle Street.** Note 'The Chantry' and 'The Hermitage' 17th century town house of Lord Bath, and no. 12, built in 1700 for Dowager Duchess of Argyll, Mistress of the Queen's Wardrobe.
2. **St John's Church.** With Via Crucis, and tomb of Bishop Ken.
3. **Cheap Street.**
4. **Market Place.** Scene in 1832 of riots during election of Frome's first M.P.
5. **Blue House.** 18th century 'Blue Coat' School, now old people's flats. Note "Nancy Guy and Billy Ball, Up against the Blue House wall".
6. **The Bridge.** Houses built on it in 1821.
7. **Catherine Hill.** Typical of Frome's medieval streets.
8. **Sheppard's Barton.** 18th century weavers' cottages built by the Sheppard family, local woollen manufacturers.
9. **Trinity Street.** Heart of Frome's Trinity area, largest collection of 17th century industrial dwellings in the county.
10. **Holy Trinity Church.** Built 1838, with stained glass windows by Burne-Jones.
11. **Bunn's Column.** Only remains of grand design by 18th century eccentric Tom Bunn for majestic boulevard to rival Bath.
12. **Bath Street.** Created by the Marquess of Bath in 1812.

SHAFTESBURY

with Gwyn Richards

I WASN'T quite prepared for my first sight of Shaftesbury. I knew it was a town on a hill, perched above the lush green Dorset countryside. But when I saw it from a distance, 700 feet above sea level on a mighty sandstone spur, it seemed to me to be a rather mysterious Jack-in-the Beanstalk sort of town, twinkling up there in the early morning sun, and for the whole day there I felt this sense of Shaftesbury's enigmatic past.

The name is derived from a unpronounceable Saxon word, Sceaftesbyrig. You try saying it and you'll see why we left it out of the script! In its lofty position, it surely must have been a prehistoric fort, but the archaeologists have found no sign of one. If that's strange, then so is the legend that it was once the site of the ancient Celtic Caer Palladwr, but once again, Shaftesbury holds on to its secrets. What is certain is that Alfred the Great built a magnificent Abbey on this hill and installed his daughter as its first Abbess.

So there I was, at the bottom of the hill, girding up my loins for the steep cobbled climb up Gold Hill. It's a good puff, but you *must* enter Shaftesbury by this marvellous mediaeval ascent.

Gold Hill isn't just Shaftesbury's pride, it's a national jewel. On the one side huge buttresses hold the town up like a giant's hand, and on the other side, thatched and tiled little cottages tumble over each other down the hill. Pause for breath as often as you like, because then you can enjoy the view across the Vale of Blackmore.

To enoy this little town and its history, do spend some time in the museum first. It's just at the top of Gold Hill set in a pleasant garden. Crammed with local interest, including the history of the Dorset button industry, centred on Shaftesbury, you will emerge well versed for the rest of your Day Out. By the way, don't miss the

SHAFTESBURY: Gold Hill

Byzant. The what? You may well ask, but the Byzant, which you should see in the museum, is like a glorified cake stand. Centuries ago it was presented in a ceremonial procession to the people of Enmore Green at the bottom of the hill. The extraordinary thing about Shaftesbury, you see, is that it had no water of its own. Enmore Green allowed them to draw water from their wells, and every drop had to be carried up the hill by hand or by donkey. The Byzant was the townspeople's odd offering in return. But that's Shaftesbury for you!

Another important feature of Shaftesbury lies behind a wall on Park Walk, a spectacular perambulation along the edge of the steep southern escarpment. Here you will find the ruins of Alfred the Great's massive Abbey, destroyed by Henry VIII. For 600 years it dominated the landscape. Here in 979, the remains of the young King Edward the Martyr were buried after his murder at Corfe Castle. Pilgrims flocked to the Abbey after miracles of healing were reported at his shrine. But his actual grave was secret, and only in recent times was a lead coffin unearthed containing the broken bones of a young man. Were they the remains of the King? We may never know, but you can still see the stone-lined grave. Legend has it that a great treasure still remains to be unearthed, because the Abbey was one of the wealthiest in the land, but all the present owner has ever found was a gold ring. You can see it in the Abbey's own museum.

After the Dissolution, the ruined Abbey became a sort of local builders' yard, and its stone crops up in walls and houses throughout the town.

As you walk along the town's narrow streets, still in their mediaeval pattern, it isn't difficult to imagine the stage coaches rattling through. Shaftesbury was the point where five turnpike roads converged. At one time there were twelve churches clustered round the Abbey; now only one remains, St Peter's in the High Street, which the Shastonians have again adopted as their Parish church. There is a strong literary connection in the town; Thomas Hardy set scenes from 'Jude the Obscure' in the Ox House along Bimport. See if for you, like me, you find it a mysterious little place, full of unexpected corners and intriguing surprises.

SHAFTESBURY

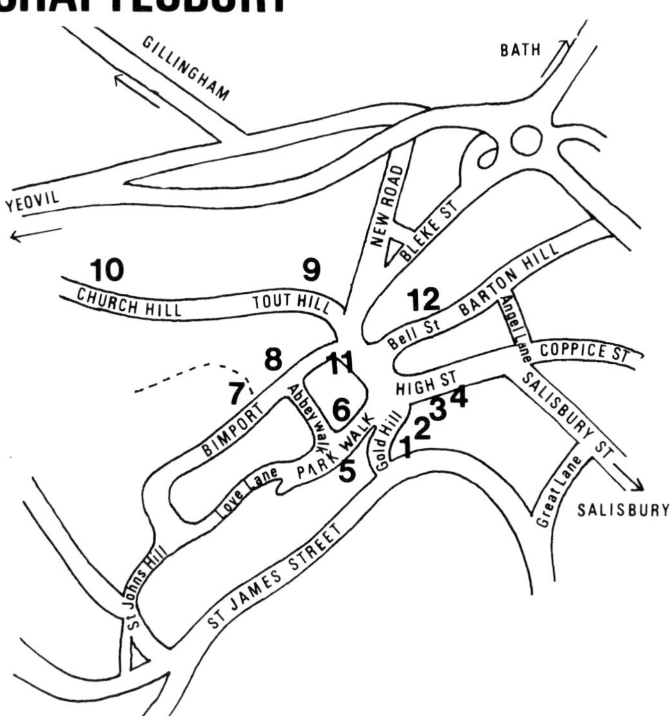

1. **Gold Mill.** Set for film 'Far from the Madding Crowd'.
2. **'Sun and the Moon'.** Former pub at top of Gold Hill where the water carriers refreshed themselves.
3. **Museum.** Selected opening times.
4. **St. Peter's Church.** Survivor of Shaftesbury's 12 medieval churches, now rehallowed parish church.
5. **Park and Abbey Walks.** High vantage point with magnificent views illustrating Shaftesbury's commanding position as hill town.
6. **Abbey.** Selected opening times.
7. **Castle Hill.** Fine views over Blackmore Vale.
8. **Ox House.** 17th century, the 'Old-Grove Place' of Thomas Hardy's 'Jude the Obscure' where Sue Bridehead fell from window without serious harm 'probably owing to the lowness of the old rooms'.
9. **Tout Hill.** Ancient thoroughfare into town.
10. **Enmore Green.** Site of springs which gave Shaftesbury its water supply.
11. **Grosvenor Hotel.** With intricately carved Chevy Chase sideboard depicting scenes from the ballad.
12. **Bell Street.** Good example of Shaftesbury's local stone houses, and tiny streets.

MALMESBURY

with Derek Jones

There I was standing like a bit of a Charlie in a tiny white-washed room with a sod of earth at my feet on which I had thrown a coin of the realm – a very small one as it happened – while I was thrashed across the shoulders with an elm twig. And there, beside me, a gentleman incanted strange words:—

"This turf and twig I give to thee.
The same as King Athelstan gave to me
And a faithful brother I hope you'll be."

That, to all intents and purposes, made me a Commoner of the Old Corporation of Malmesbury, but it didn't mean I could go dashing off to the local common land and plant my spuds, graze a herd of cows or look forward to a rich harvest of barley. No. Like other parcels of land elsewhere in the country, some are more common than others, and this particular parcel is far from common. Not to put too fine a point on it, it's very select and common but to a few. I didn't really think I should get my portion even after the strange initiation ceremony, because when these folk drew up their rules they thoughtfully included clauses – like the small print on a present day insurance contract that so few of us read until it's too late – clauses that make very certain that any Tom, Dick or Derek can't elbow in on the act. I wasn't even on the starting line. I wasn't a Freeman, I wasn't a resident householder. So on two minor counts my visions of sharing the nearly 600 acres of King's Heath fell by the wayside.

King's Heath is nothing to write home about, just a flat expanse of agricultural land lying a couple of miles out of the town, but that acreage is about three times the area of the town itself and that puts it into perspective. It's a very worthwhile piece of property. You very soon realise as you walk around Malmesbury that the townsfolk seem to be carrying on a bit of high powered publicity for Athelstan,

MALMESBURY: Abbey (West Front)

the name crops up everywhere on all sorts of unlikely enterprises, and then, with a jerk, you remember a line in that incantation when you almost became a commoner. "The same as King Athelstan gave to me." Athelstan is revered hereabouts. It seems that he was so grateful for assistance he received from the local men in his battle with the Danes that he granted them the gift of the common land, King's Heath, for ever. And for ever it has remained so far. Not a bad tribute to the solidarity of our way of life that more than a thousand years should have passed and nothing has changed. Actually it has changed in one small measure in that the commoners no longer trek out from town to till the soil and harvest the crops. All that came to an end in wartime days when the War Ag. took charge of the common in the battle to make the country self-sufficient and since then the commoners have found it more beneficial to let the land to local farmers and divide the proceeds of the rent among themselves. Mind you, no one is saying what the income is these days, but it has to be divided up according to tradition among the commoners, 280 of them, the 52 acresmen (lovely word that means just what it says, men entitled to an acre of land for life), the 24 assistant burgesses, 12 capital burgesses and the man who takes the chair at their court meetings, the High Steward.

Malmesbury is dominated by the Abbey or at least by what is left of it, and once again we find ourselves rubbing shoulders with the grandson of Alfred the Great, for Athelstan's tomb is here in this great Norman structure. It's staggering in its splendour, but what it must have been like in its greater days only the imagination can tell. We're told that the whole monastic establishment originally covered some 45 acres and the east end of the Abbey used to be far, far beyond the present wall and you get some idea of just how enormous the Abbey must have been. Incidentally, you won't get in many cricket pitches into your walk before you come against garden walls, but out

MALMESBURY

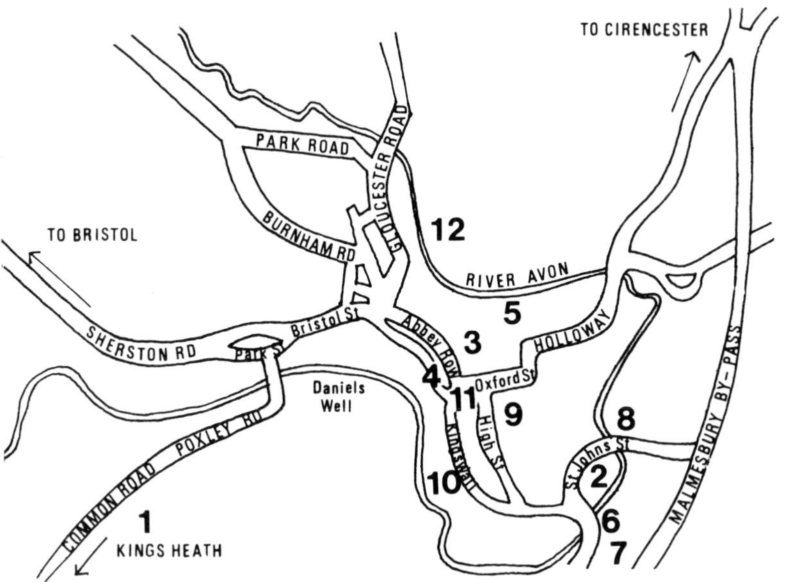

. **King's Heath.** (Or Common land approx. 2 miles out of town.) Given to the Commoners of Malmesbury by King Athelstan over a thousand years ago.

. **Old Court House.** A 13th century relic today used by the Old Corporation (formed from the Commoners) for its ceremonies.

. **Abbey.** Impressive remains of this Norman building now parish church. Outstanding feature is the south porch : burial place of King Athelstan.

. **Athelstan Museum.** Houses many items of local interest, including Malmesbury lace – a cottage industry here in the 18th century.

. **Abbey House.** Originally Abbot's residence stood here. Present house built in 16th century by a cloth merchant. Now occupied by the Deaconness Order of St. Andrew.

6. **Almshouses.** The Hospital of St. John almshouses for poor widows.
7. **Old Silk Mill.** Standing nearby on St. John's Bridge this mill once provided silk for a London store – now an antique shop.
8. **Goose Bridge.** Herds of geese used to be driven across this bridge to the meadows below.
9. **Cross Hayes.** Originally the market square – good car parking facilities here.
10. **King's Wall.** Walk along this pathway to King's Walk, or 'Tupenny tube'.
11. **Market Cross.** Described as one of the finest market crosses in the country it provides a good central meeting place.
12. **River Walk.** Pleasant river walk almost encircles town.

beyond them was the old Abbey east end. The Nave to-day is but a third of its original length.

Malmesbury has so much to offer, so many quaint bits of history that I found even a couple of days filming on location wasn't enough to take it all in, we just creamed the surface of the history, tradition and legend. It was patently a town where the weavers grew rich, first on wool and then on silk, and built their elegant homes; where the cottage industry was lace-making, when women sat in their tiny windows to get as much light as possible on their delicate work, and ruined their eyesight in the process.

Malmesbury lace became rightly famous in the 18th century, and to-day we can see examples of it in the Museum, beautiful work. Sadly, there are very few people left to-day with the craft at their fingertips. But what wouldn't I give for an evening dress shirt edged with Malmesbury lace.

The town stands proudly on high ground, almost surrounded by water, the River Avon and its tributaries and knowing my interest in natural history, the film crew knew where to find me on the summer days when we were there. If Derek was missing he was listening to the superb bird-song in the Abbey churchyard and the gardens around it, or looking deep into the water of the river. What they didn't realise was that I was listening for the shrill whistle or hoping to catch a glimpse of a darting flash of blue under one of the many bridges in the town. The local ornithologists told me they had quite a few kingfishers along those waters. I didn't see a single one, but I'll be back, not only to look for them, but also for so much else I missed. It's the sort of town, Malmesbury, that wants you to come back, and I for one, received that message, as loud and clear as the whistle of a kingfisher.

CLEARWELL

with Derek Jones

YOUR first reaction on seeing the tiny sprawl of cottages down the hill past the Castle and the Church, hard by the Wyndham Arms, is one of wonder. Wonder not at the beauty or the character for neither are there in any great evidence, but wonder at what on earth happened to make a community spring up here, in the backwoods, in the first place. Just down the road from the Wyndham Arms (excellent food here by the way – always important for an ever hungry film crew) is a long narrow building, leaning with creaking age. This was the nail factory and the nails are made of iron, mined in the locality. And once you've equated Clearwell with iron the picture unfolds.

Just up the hill above the village lives a gentle elderly giant of a farmer, Mostyn Watkins by name. He keeps a few beef cattle in his fields by the old pear orchard, but I get the feeling he keeps his eyes more on his wood than his stock. It's just behind the orchard, this wood covering some 15 acres. Just like any other small wood with a few cherry trees, lots of yew and sycamore, beech and rowan. That's the impression from the outside, but go through the neat wicket gate into its bowels and you're in another world. It's eerie inside, trees cutting out what little light there is on a dull day, with a winding meandering path that takes you deeper and deeper into the dark depths, through minature Cheddar Gorges, up and down steep steps worn out of the rock. Here is the beginning of the story of iron for this old wood, known as Perry-Grove Wood or more graphically, Puzzlewood, is really the raped remains of open-cast iron workings. Even before Roman times iron was worked here and the Romans naturally carried on. Then as the iron was worked out Nature, the great restorer of blots on the landscape, took over and re-clothed these scowls. For Mostyn Watkins the wood is a way of life. He delights in taking you around, his eyes twinkling as he tells you to stay close or you'll get lost. You could too if he weren't with you in this maze of paths among the trees and tiny chasms. And if you need convincing of his love of the wood just think of the work involved in keeping the paths tidy and clear of leaves throughout the year. Mostyn does it all himself.

If I were an intrepid pot-holer, which I most definitely am not, I could have made my way underground from a cave entrance on Mostyn's land to another complex of iron workings close by Clearwell. These came later when man had taken all the iron ore he could by digging on the surface and had to go down. So to Old Ham Mines, or Clearwell Caves as they're known to-day. There's still iron ore down there to-day, and indeed it was still in production less than 30 years ago.

Ray Wright owns the mines to-day, and he is like Mostyn Watkins in many ways in that he's a bit of a loner, busy trying to find all the old passages and big caverns that are still down there hundreds of feet below the rugged hills. He's come across quite a few relics of the old mining days in the course of his excavations, and what more natural than to put them to good use. Clearwell Caves is taking shape as a museum of Forest of Dean mining, and in Ray Wright it has an enthusiast who knows the 2,000 year history of mining in the area like no-one else. And what is more he not only likes to talk about it, but talks with a quiet humour. I shall always remember his story of the miners with missing thumbs. Get him to tell it if you can. As I understand it extracting the ore was a two man business, or rather man and boy. The boy held an iron bar over his shoulder as the man hit the bar with a heavy hammer. Because of the noise communication between the two was difficult and if the boy wanted a rest he flashed his thumb over the end of the iron bar on his shoulder. You can imagine the rest. Quite a few thumbs came to grief that way among the

CLEARWELL CASTLE

Forest of Dean miners.

They're tough these Forest folk. Perhaps it's because of the harsh environment in which they find themselves, and it seems to get into the system of outsiders who've come in and become one of them. Like Alice Yeates. But I'm ahead of myself.

Clearwell Castle looks down on the village, a large Gothic style building. It was put up over a period of years in the early 18th century and after a fire in 1929, restoration and then deterioration it stood gaunt and empty. That brings us to the early fifties. But back again a few years. Frank Yeates was the son of the gardener at the Castle. Frank was born in 1913 and while he was a youngster the family moved north.

Then in 1953 Frank Yeates heard of the sad plight of the old castle, and to cut a long story short, he and his wife, Alice, paid a visit to Clearwell. They bought the ruin and with their own hands they set about restoring the place, the biggest Do-it-Yourself operation I have ever seen. My own efforts go no further than a modest bit of amateur paper hanging, but imagine re-roofing a castle, putting in new flooring, making mouldings to fit in with decayed and rotting ceilings. Alice and Frank did it and they soon found that they had friends. Mysteriously odds and ends of fittings from the Castle, long since missing began to re-appear.

To-day, Alice, now a widow, runs the castle as a tourist attraction with the help of members of her family, only too glad to show you around, or of an evening organise a baronial banquet. That's the sort of determination that is part of the character of the Forest of Dean where men pride their independence and jealously guard their rights as Commoners. It's a pity we weren't all so endowed.

CLEARWELL

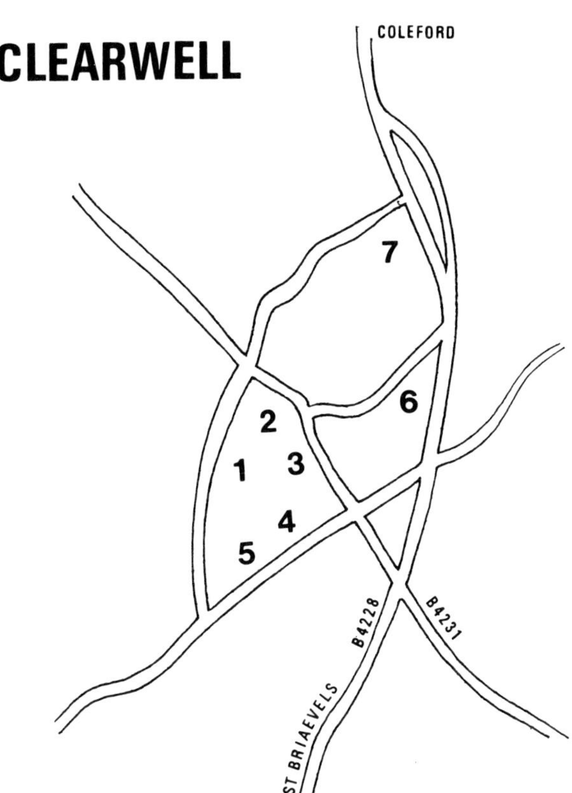

- **Castle.** A castle saved from ruin by a big Do-It-Yourself exercise making an Englishman's house the gardener's son's castle. (Open to public most days.)
- **The Clearwell.** A well with glorious supply of fresh water from under the Forest of Dean hills. Has never been known to dry up.
- **Village Cross.** An attractive old cross in middle of village made of stones reinforced with iron straps.
- **Wyndham Arms.** Attractive 16/17th century building with over-hanging timber-framed gable and mullioned windows.

5. **Parish Church.** Designed by John Middleton for the Countess Dunraven.
6. **Old Ham Mine.** Iron mines closed after 1st world war. Now fast becoming a museum of forest mining. (Open to public most days.)
7. **Scowles.** Remains of massive open cast iron ore excavations left from Roman times; now heavily vegetated, providing beautifully sheltered walks over 15 acres.
   Situated at Perrygrove Farm and the owner, Mostyn Watkins, welcomes visitors at any reasonable hour . . . and a contribution to church funds.

CLEVEDON

with Gwyn Richards

GO ON, blow those cobwebs away! Stand on the cliffs at Clevedon, fill your lungs with fresh air. It's invigorating, makes you want to kick your heels in the air, (not too close to the edge, though)! It was just that feeling of bounding health, which a good sniff at the Atlantic breezes can give you, that our ancestors craved. George IV led the fashionable flight to the seaside and made Brighton what it is today. So the rich merchants of Bristol and Bath beat a path to the tiny hamlets on the estuary of the Severn. In only twenty years, from the beginning of the 19th Century, Clevedon grew from a few cottages round the village green and a lonely parish church on the cliffs, to a thriving Regency and Victorian resort, with two fine stone built hotels and a nucleus of grand houses, many of which stand today.

Well, when we were in Clevedon, it was blowing a gale! But yes, I loved the place.

Now, take the beautiful Poets Walk pathway along the cliffs to St Andrew's, the 13th century church perched high above the sea, and strangely remote from the town. Built on Celtic foundations, with many mediaeval features still preserved, it surely must be the most dramatically situated parish church in England. It may well have been used as a beacon church to guide shipping in the Channel. It is also the burial place of the young Arthur Hallam who, before his sudden death in Vienna, formed a deep friendship with the poet Tennyson. It was seventeen years before the Poet Laureate could find the courage to visit the grave. He wrote his famous elegy, 'In Memoriam', as a tribute to Hallam.

Another path, Lover's Walk, winds along to Ladye Bay the other side of the town, where there are more views of the Channel, the 'dim coasts and cloudlike hills' of Coleridge's poem about the scene. Up high on the

CLEVEDON: Pier

nearby golf course, you can also wander around the 17th Century ruins of Walton Castle.

The great tragedy of Clevedon, of course, is the ruin of its graceful Victorian iron pier. In 1970, two vital spans of this classic construction, described as the finest in England, slipped unprotestingly into the sea. Opened on

Easter Monday, 1869, the pier only just survived its own centenary, while being tested for its continued safety for public use. A fund was raised to restore it, but so far these hopes have not been realised.

In Clevedon itself, take your time. Dawdle along the various premises and up above, notice the upper storeys and roof lines, many of which are fine legacies from Clevedon's first beginnings as a graceful 19th Century residence of the prosperous. In the side roads, too, take in the splendid Victorian villas, and see how easily you can imagine the scene a hundred years ago, top hats, parasols and full length dresses.

There are two centres in Clevedon; the 19th Century garden resort, with its network of delightful paths, and the more commercial shopping and business centre clustered round the clock tower about a mile from the sea front. This, curiously enough, is where you'll find two of Clevedon's most historic literary and architectural features. First, along the main road, set back in its rose garden and lawn, is the tiny cottage where the poet Samuel Taylor Coleridge spent his honeymoon in 1795. He had married a young Bristol girl, Sara Fricker, and even then there were roses, for he described how the tallest 'peeped at the chamber window. We could hear at silent noon and eve and early morn, the sea's faint murmur.'

No chance of that today, I'm afraid. Too much traffic noise for one thing. And at the great Clevedon Court, not far away, the traffic thundering by along the M5. motorway, also tends to disturb the peace. Probably the oldest domestic house in England, and occupied since 1709 by the Elton family, it was associated with another literary figure of Victorian times, William Makepeace Thackeray. Walk along its terraced gardens and reflect on your day out in Clevedon, a town which, to our profit, clings happily to its description of a Victorian arcadia. And it does your lungs good, too!

CLEVEDON

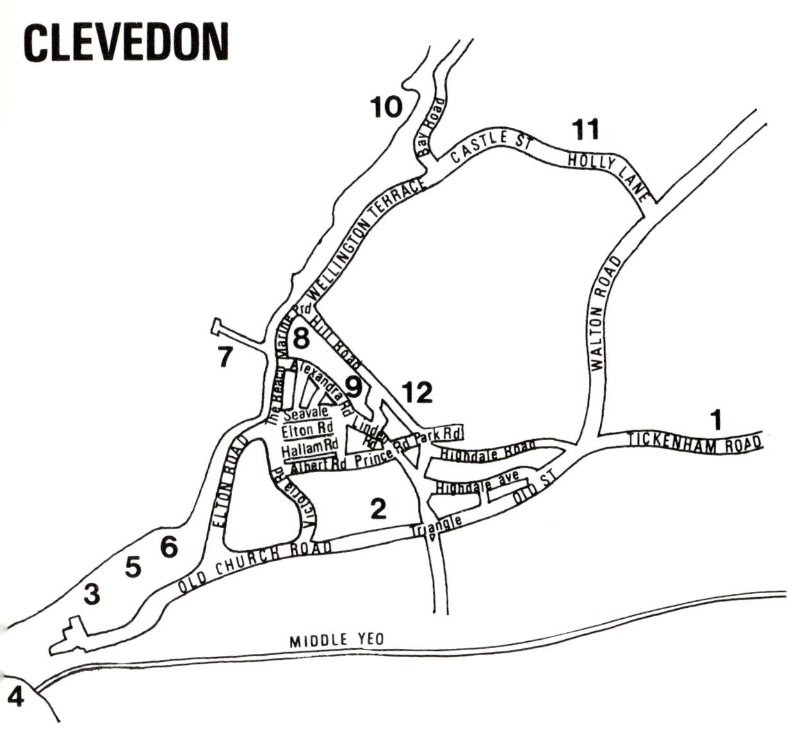

Clevedon Court. National Trust, selected opening times.
Coleridge's Cottage. Privately owned, plaque on wall.
Church of St. Andrew.
The Pill. Tidal inlet once used to bring coal in from Wales.
Church Hill. Impressive view of Victorian Clevedon.
Marine Lake and amusement park.
Pier.
Royal Hotel and Marine Hotel. Clevedon's first hotels built in 1820s, now Franciscan Friary, and St. Antony's School.

9. **Hill Road.** Start of Clevedon's development as Victorian resort, with variety of styles to be found in immediate area.
10. **Ladye Bay.** Popular with gentlemen bathers in last century.
11. **Walton Castle.** Possibly built as a hunting lodge by Lord Poulett around 1615.
12. **Dial Hill.** Clevedon's highest point, best reached by zig zag path from Hill Road, with fine views over channel.

LANGPORT

with Derek Jones

OUT here on the great green flat expanse of the Somerset levels, high ground is as scarce as salmon in the River Thames and any piece of land that rears its head out of the winter floods could rightly be called an island, or even a hill. Here at Langport there's treasure indeed; not just one piece of relatively high ground, but two. Indeed there's a pass, though if we stuck it down in Cheddar Gorge we'd hardly even notice it. So there just had to be a settlement here, a place where defenders could look out and actually just see over their attackers heads. The advantages were obvious and besides which any army encamped here was pretty safe in the knowledge that an attack had to come their way since here was one of the few places where the river could be crossed.

The River is the Parret which, down the centuries, has been both frontier and highway, although to-day as it flows sluggishly on its way to Bridgwater and the open sea, you'd think it hadn't the energy to make it. Indeed at times you can look down into it and find yourself wondering which way it is actually flowing so lethargic is its progress. But in truth it goes both ways, since it's tidal like the Severn, and boasts a bore, though let it be said with none of the majesty and sheer brute grandeur of the walls of water that rush up the Severn on those high spring tides with a sou-westerly wind pushing them along.

I started my day out on the banks of the Parret just outside the town. It was a Sunday morning. The splendid spires and towers of the churches around—and in this part of Somerset there is some of the finest ecclesiastical architecture I've seen anywhere—stood up out of the mists to beckon the faithful. From one at Huish Episcopi we could even hear the peal of bells. Those bells though fell on many a deaf ear out there on the banks of the Parret for here men, and one or two women for that matter, had

LANGPORT: Hanging Chapel

other things in mind apart from the good of their souls. There they were, a yard or so apart, along the river banks under great awnings of umbrellas, quietly casting their lines out, for the Parret has some very fine coarse fishing, not only for the members of the local clubs, but for many people from other parts of the country who make annual pilgrimages to join in the sport.

There's one walk in the town I found slightly disconcerting, along the main thoroughfare that leads straight as a die to the splendid bridge over the river, down where Westover Station used to be. (Langport's a bit like that, with lots of 'used to be' about its character.) This walk along Bow Street though could upset the equilibrium. There you go, quietly looking at the shop and house fronts with many an old arch to allow access to stable yards, and others made into shop windows, and you suddenly think the world is going slightly on the tilt. I found myself lining up the side of one old building with something of more recent construction just to make sure I wasn't seeing things. It was I hasten to add, the time of day when not a drop had passed by lips. And sure enough there is something wrong. Many of the buildings lean backwards. The locals will soon explain the problem. The fronts of them are on the good foundations of the old Causeway leading to the river crossing but behind them, down where the garden paths begin, is the edge of the low-lying moors where even in dry times the water table is never far beneath your feet.

Over the years those buildings have tended to sag into the soft ground. So don't worry! And don't worry about some of the strange roofs so plentiful around the town, distinctive in having two slopes to them, the lower one steeper than the upper. This is nothing to do with subsidence, but a bit of continental design: Mansard roofs that probably crept into the town when the river was an important waterway with its own docks from where barges discharged cargo to supply the whole of central Somerset.

It goes without saying that I saw and marvelled at the strange Hanging Chapel hard by the parish church; at the nearby church of Huish Episcopi and at the little church at Muchelney, cheek by jowl with the Abbey. When Muchelney really was a 'big island' as its name implies, it's not hard to see that a monastic establishment would be pretty safe out there surrounded by flood water.

LANGPORT

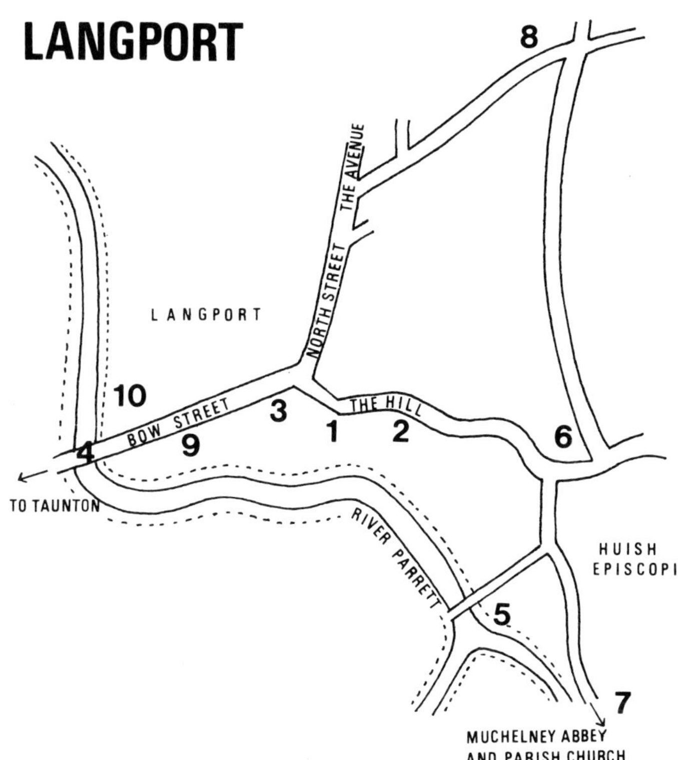

1. **Langport Church:** (All Saints.) Here lies Langport's most famous son, Economist Walter Bagehot.
2. **Hanging Chapel.** So called because of its strange hanging position at one entrance to town.
3. **Bank House.** Birthplace of Walter Bagehot.
4. **River Bridge.** A crossing point from mediaeval times.
5. **Yeo Corner.** Meeting place of anglers.
6. **Huish Episcopi.** St. Mary's church with its beautiful tower and peal of bells.
7. **Muchelney Abbey and Parish Church.** Abbey ruins – Benedictine monks established here by King Ino. Adjacent is parish church containing stones and 13th century tiles from Abbey. Abbey ruins open to public all year round.
8. **Kelways Nurseries.** An old established industry in town. To rear of nursery is the wildfowl park (privately owned).
9. **Bow Street.** Houses with Mansard roofs. Built on a causeway, buildings in this street tend to lean backwards towards moorland.
10. **River Walk.** In two directions, from River Bridge (4).

RIVER FROME

with Gwyn Richards

'The Deluge at Bristol: A Third of the City Submerged: Several miles of houses and shops wrecked: River Froom a Raging Torrent!' Read all about it!

So screamed the *Bristol Observer's* headlines in March 1889. A strange way, perhaps for me to begin to write about a Day Out down the River Frome (as it's spelt today). But my stroll along this infamous river *was* something of a history lesson. It isn't a very long river, less than twenty miles, in fact, and although your outing along it may need a couple of hops from place to place, you will begin to understand why it gave Bristol so much trouble around a hundred years ago.

To see the River Frome at its source, you must go to Dodington House, the home of the Codrington family just off the M4 near Bath. In the grounds, landscaped by Capability Brown, you will find the river above the house trickling quietly down to the tranquil lakes it forms in front of this Georgian mansion.

The architect James Wyatt cunningly used the clear water in the service of man. Under the house, in the cellars which are now used as a restaurant, the water emerges in a stone trough. Ale was made here, and the running stream water also provided the house with a highly efficient sewage system, still in use today, which carefully emptied *below* the lakes in the most efficaceous way!

You may want to spend a little time at Dodington, but then our journey takes us along the A432, via Chipping Sodbury and Yate, aiming eventually for our next stop, the picturesque village of Frenchay. Here, surprisingly, we find another Dodington-like landscape, far removed from what you might expect from the edge of a big city. But Frenchay is lucky.

It was always rather remote, saving it from the urban

RIVER FROME: Snuff Mills Park

RIVER FROME

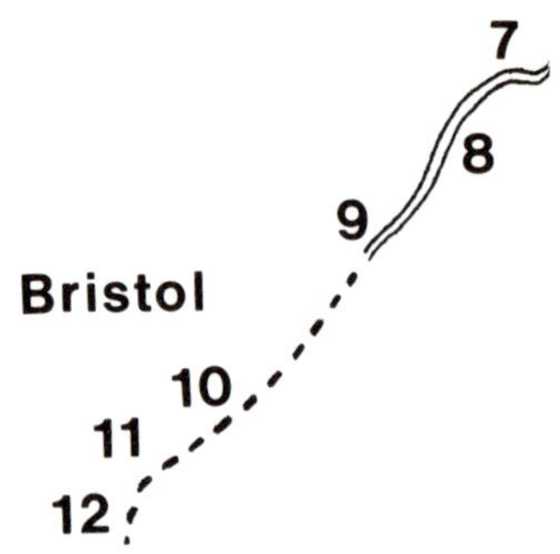

1. **Seven Springs.** Source of Frome in Dodington Park.
2. **Dodington House.** Frome diverted under house to provide running water – well in cellars.
3. **Dodington Park.** 1764 Capability Brown landscaped park, damming Frome to create interconnecting lakes.
4. **Iron Action.** Attractive Fromeside village.
5. **Bury Hill.** Site of iron age fort with ramparts still visible.
6. **Frenchay.** (See other map.)
7. **Snuff Mills Park.** Attractive riverside walk and nature trail with working water wheel near entrance and remains of other mills visible.
8. **Eastville Park.** Riverside walk continues from Snuff Mills to Eastville Park.
9. **Northern Storm Water Inte ceptor.** Completed in 1962 to div Frome flood waters by means of hu drain across north Bristol into Av Gorge.
10. **Centre.** River covered over in 18
11. **Neptune Statue.** Frome kept fr entering Floating Harbour by flo gates under Centre.
12. **Mylnes Culvert.** 1828 Fro diverted from Centre and empti into Avon near Bathhurst basin culvert visible at low tide.

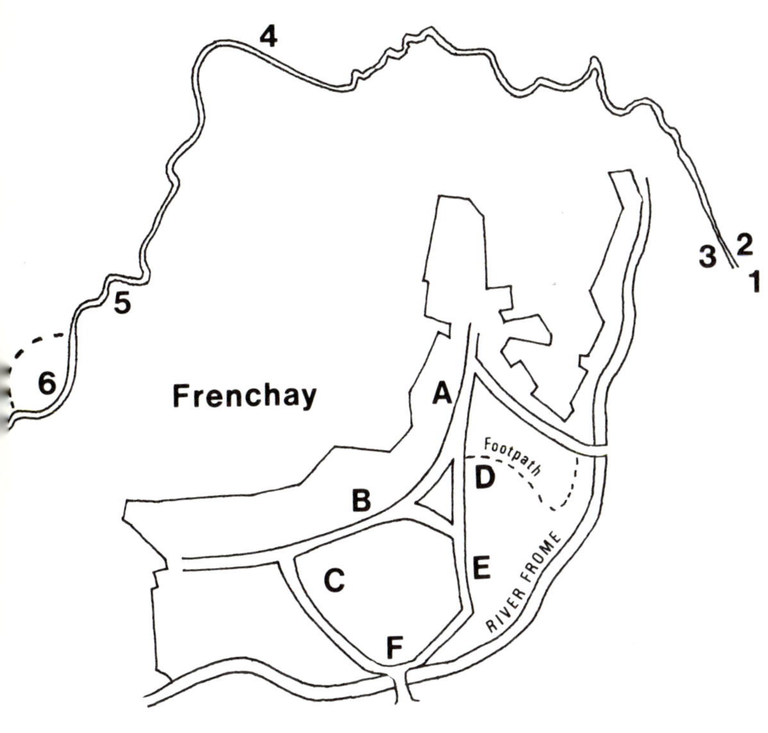

Friends Meeting House. With graveyard at the rear of the building.

Unitarian Chapel. 1720 – note graverobbers stone in corner of graveyard.

Frenchay Common. W. G. Grace played cricket here: 1870 captain Frenchay Cricket Club. Backdrop of Georgian houses.

D. **Frenchay Fields.** Excellent walk from Cleve bridge across fields to Frenchay Common showing Frenchay's rural character.

E. **Frenchay Village.** Narrow streets with village Post Office and stores and clustered cottages.

F. **Frenchay Bridge.** Nearby disused quarry and entrance to Snuff Mills Park.

sprawl. Over 300 years ago it was refuge for religious dissenters from the laws of worship of the Church of England. The Quakers, for instance, felt safe enough here to build their first meeting house in Frenchay, in 1673. Their present house was built on the same site, by the Green.

You may visit this quiet meeting room, and walk round the old garden where Quakers are buried, including J. S. Fry, founder of the chocolate firm, and his wife Ann. Over the wall is a huge tulip tree planted, it's thought, by William Penn, founder of Pennsylvania.

In later years Frenchay always seemed to attract the more prosperous. W. G. Grace captained Frenchay cricket club, but as you walk down the hill, past the Post Office, you find the other Frenchay, the little village where they dug Pennant stone. Quarrymen's cottages tumble down the hill, and in one place, a quarry has formed an attractive garden. And here is the river again, crossed by the old stone bridge. Now you can see why the river became such a bully. Frome is a Saxon name meaning rapid. In two and a half miles it drops fifty feet. In heavy rain, it would become a torrent down this gorge, and all those downstream, watch out!

You can walk to Snuff Mills, our next stop, down the path, or drive the short distance. But along this riverside walk you can enjoy truly idyllic surroundings, and reflect that you're actually inside the city boundary. In collaboration with the City Parks department, the Bristol Naturalists' Society created a nature reserve through this valley, and here also is the last of the water wheels left over from early industry, when snuff was ground for the Wills factory. This is a green lung in the heart of a city, safe for children to play, and here the river loses itself.

You can call it a day at Snuff Mills if you like. But should you still be curious about the Frome, find your way to Neptune's statue in Bristol's centre. Look back towards the Cenotaph and imagine the scene as a bustling dockland, with tall ships moored at Narrow Quay. Here the Frome became almost a running sewer, a long battle which ended with it being completely covered over. Millions of pounds has been spent to funnel it away out of danger, so that no more floods shall deluge the city. It has a rather sorry end, emptying itself not in the floating harbour, as many believe, but from an outfall into the Avon.

An old adversary tamed.

ABSON BOOKS

A SHOCKING HISTORY OF BRISTOL – 70p by Derek Robinson. An accurate account of Bristol's White Slavery, Quaker Bashing, Civil War, Black Slavery, Riots and Port Scandals.

BRISTOL DIALECT BOOKS: Krek Waiter's Peak Bristle 55p; Son of Bristle 55p; Bristle Rides Again 55p; Sick Sundered Yers of Bristle 36p.

EATING OUT IN BRISTOL & BATH – 60p – A selection of restaurants and pubs recommended by local residents who were asked where they enjoyed eating out.

COOKERY BOOKS: Cooking Courgettes 50p; Cooking Broccoli & Cauliflower 45p; Cooking Aubergines 50p; Cooking Carrots 50p; Cooking Spinach 50p.

LANGUAGE GLOSSARIES: Rhyming Cockney Slang 50p; American/English 50p; Scottish/English 50p; Australian/English 50p.

OTHER ABSON BOOKS:
English Delft Tiles 55p; A Guide to Hip Language & Culture 35p; How Not to Do Your Duty 36p; Get Golf Straight 45p.

ABSON BOOKS

All available from booksellers or by adding 10p for the first copy and 3p per copy thereafter for packing and postage from the publishers.
Abson Books, Abson, Wick, Bristol BS15 5TT.

Printed by Burleigh Ltd., Bristol